HOW TO CODE

A STEP-BY-STEP GUIDE TO COMPUTER CODING

1 2 3 4

Max Wainewright

Q Quarto Library

Internet safety

Children should be supervised when using the internet, particularly when using an unfamiliar website for the first time.

Children can learn HTML and JavaScript without sharing their work online. Before uploading anything to the web, please read the advice about e-safety on page 26.

The publisher and author cannot be held responsible for the content of the websites referred to in this book.

Quarto is the authority on a wide range of topics.

Quarto educates, entertains and enriches the lives of our readers—enthusiasts and lovers of hands-on living.

www.quartoknows.com

Design: Angela and Dave Ball, Mike Henson
Illustration: Mike Henson
Editor: Claudia Martin
Project Editor: Carly Madden
Consultant: Sean McManus
Editorial Director: Victoria Garrard
Art Director: Laura Roberts-Jensen

This edition published in 2017 by Quarto Library., an imprint of QEB Publishing, Inc.

First published in library binding in 2015

6 Orchard, Lake Forest, CA 92630

Distributed in the United States and Canada by Lerner Publisher Services
241 First Avenue North
Minneapolis, MN 55401 U.S.A.
www.lernerbooks.com

A CIP record for the book is available from the Library of Congress.

ISBN 978 1 68297 079 9

Printed in China

JavaScript was originally developed in 1995 by Brendan Eich while working for the Netscape Communications Corporation.

CONTENTS :: BOOK 4

Enter

INTRODUCTION

You probably use the World Wide Web every day to find out information, check out the news, or download music. In this book, you will find out how web pages are built and learn to create your own web pages using HTML and JavaScript.

What is the web?

Computers can be connected together by cables and, often, by wireless links. Computers that are connected together are called a **network**. A network can be used to share information and resources.

The internet is a global network of computers. It is used for things like the web, email, and downloading music.

The World Wide Web (or web for short) uses the internet to share web pages.

Key word

Internet: An enormous network of computers connected across the whole world.

Did you know?

The web was invented by the British computer scientist Tim Berners-Lee in 1989.

Getting around the web

All pages on the web have their own special address so that we can go straight to them when we need them—sort of like a mailing address takes mail straight to the right house on the right street. The address is called a **URL**, which stands for Uniform Resource Locator. Pages are often linked together with **hyperlinks**. Clicking on these links takes us from one page to another.

Browser
//desktop/favorites/index.html
http://www.google.com/

What is HTTP?

All things that use the internet have to obey their own set of rules for how to share information. If they didn't, everyone would be doing things in a different way and we wouldn't all be able to share information across the world. These rules are called **protocols**. The protocol used for the World Wide Web is called the Hypertext Transfer Protocol (HTTP). You have probably seen the letters "http" at the start of web addresses. HTTP is the standard way to transport web pages over the internet.

What is HTML?

Web pages are written in a special language or code called HTML (Hypertext Markup Language). This book will teach you how to use HTML to make your own pages.

Text editor—headings.html

```html
<html>
  <h1>London</h1>
  <p>England</p>
  <h1>Paris</h1>
  <p>France</p>
</html>
```

JavaScript

This book will also teach you how to add JavaScript to your web pages. JavaScript is a programming language that you can use within a web page to make it more interactive.

```javascript
<script>
  for(var n=1; n<10; n++)
    document.write(n);
</script>
```

Key word

World Wide Web: A system that uses the internet to connect pages of information from around the world.

What is a server?

To share the web pages you create over the internet, you would need to load them onto a special computer called a server. But don't worry: to learn to create web pages, you just need to work on a normal desktop computer or laptop. You can keep your web pages private for now!

What is a browser?

In order to look at a web page, we need to use a special program called a browser. Popular browsers include Chrome, Firefox, Internet Explorer, and Safari. A browser uses HTTP to access web pages and then interprets the code in the HTML to display the web pages on our computer screen.

CREATING WEB PAGES

If you want to make a page of information that can be shown online, you need to write it using a code, or language, called HTML. We need to use a program called a text editor to write our HTML and a browser to view it in.

HTML uses tags

To show what goes on a web page we use special codes called tags.

Tags always have angle brackets < > around them.

The page must start with an **opening HTML** tag.

Text editor—mypage.html

```
<html>
        My web page
</html>
```

Everything between the tags is HTML.

The closing tag has a slash: **/**

It ends with a **closing HTML** tag.

Now get started!

To get started, we are going to make some simple web pages. You can store them on your computer instead of on the internet. This will make it quicker and safer to test and try out ideas.

You will need a text editor and a web browser to do this. See page 31 for help on finding them. You will probably already have a **web browser** on your computer. This is the program you use to view pages on the web.

A text editor is a special kind of word processor, a little like the program you use to type a story or a letter. You probably already have one on your computer: **Notepad** on a PC, and **TextEdit** on a Mac.

Key word

Tags: Special words used to describe what objects there are on a web page.

Create a web page on your computer

1

ON A WINDOWS COMPUTER

Click: **"Start," "Programs," "Accessories," "Notepad"**

For Windows 8: At the top right of the screen, click **"Search,"** type **"Notepad,"** then click the program.

ON A MAC

Click **"Spotlight"** 🔍 (top right of the screen)

Type **textedit** | Spotlight textedit |

Press **"Enter"**

2

If you are using a Mac, you need to make sure the page is being saved in the right way before you start. Click the TextEdit **"Preferences"** menu then click **"Plain text"** and uncheck **"Smart quotes."**

Turn to page 31 for extra help doing this.

3

Type your web page in your text editor. Click **"File"** then **"Save"** to save it on your desktop as **mypage.html**.

Text editor – mypage.html

```
<html>
    My web page
</html>
```

Type the <, > and / carefully!

4

On your desktop, double-click your file to open it in a web browser, on your computer:

mypage.html

Browser
//desktop/mypage.html ↻

My web page

Help!

If you can't find your **mypage.html** file, think about where you saved it. If you still can't find it, start again from step 1 and try saving your file on the desktop. Then move the text editor to one side (by dragging the title) so you can see the file on the desktop.

Make sure you save your file as **mypage.html** not mypage.txt. It's very important to get the right extension (html not txt). If you get the wrong extension or no extension at all, check that "Hide extension" and "If no extension provided, use txt" are not ticked when you save.

USING HTML

We are going to take a look in more detail at an HTML page. Each object on the page has a special tag to tell the page what it is. We are going to learn about how to use different tags.

h1 means heading.

P means paragraph.

Making headings

1

Open up your text editor. For instructions, turn back to page 7.

2

In your text editor, type:

Text editor
```
<html>
    <h1>My story</h1>
    <p>Once upon a time</p>
</html>
```

3

Save your file as **headings.html**.

4

headings.html

Find your file and double-click it.

5

You should now see your page looking like this:

Browser
//desktop/headings.html

My story

Once upon a time

Arrange your desktop so you have your text editor on the left of the screen and your web browser on the right. This will make it easier for you to experiment and see the effects.

Text editor—headings.html
```
<html>
    <h1>My short story</h1>
    <p>Once upon a time</p>
</html>
```

Browser
//desktop/headings.html

My short story

Once upon a time

Try changing a few words. Then click "File" and "Save."

Press the "Refresh" button to see changes.

Other tags

There are lots of tags you can use within normal text to emphasize certain words or to create different types of headings. Try adding some of these tags on your page. Remember to put opening tags before the words you want to change. Spend some time making small changes, saving, and refreshing your page each time.

Tag	Description	Example	Appearance
<h1>	Main heading	<h1>Europe</h1>	**Europe**
<h3>	Minor heading	<h3>United Kingdom</h3>	**United Kingdom**
<strong>	Strong text (bold)	It was <strong>very</strong> tasty.	It was **very** tasty.
<em>	Emphasized text (italic)	It was <em>very</em> tasty.	It was *very* tasty.
<mark>	Highlighted text	10 20 <mark>30</mark> 40 50 60	10 20 30 40 50 60

Now try these

Try typing in the HTML below. Save and refresh to see how each page looks.
Then check the answers on page 30.

1 Text editor—headings.html

```
<html>
    <h1>Cyber Cafe</h1>
    <p>Open every day</p>
</html>
```

2 Text editor—headings.html

```
<html>
    <h1>Code School</h1>
    <h2>Smith Street</h2>
    <p>Learn to code</p>
</html>
```

3 Text editor—headings.html

```
<html>
    <h1>Huge</h1>
    <h3>Medium</h3>
    <h5>Tiny</h5>
</html>
```

4 Text editor—headings.html

```
<html>
    <h1>London</h1>
    <p>England</p>
    <h1>Paris</h1>
    <p>France</p>
</html>
```

It doesn't matter how you line up or "indent" your HTML code. In this book, we show our HTML code with indents to make it easier to read. Most coders do this when writing web pages.

Make sure your file name ends in **.html** or it won't work!

ADDRESSES AND LINKS

Deliver. WHERE?!?

DELIVERY

Every page on the web has its own address. Most pages also have hyperlinks. Clicking one of these links takes you to another page or another website. We are going to find out how addresses and hyperlinks work.

Understanding web addresses

Just as every house has its own address, each page on the web has its own special address—a URL.

URL means Uniform Resource Locator.

Browser

◀ ▶ www.mysite.com/mypage.html

My web page

Each part of the address tells us something about the page and where it is:

www.mysite.com/mypage.html

Most web pages start with www.

The website is probably based in the United States.

The page is called mypage.

The page type is HTML.

Web addresses around the world

The part of the URL before the slash **/** is called the domain. The last part of the domain tells us where the page is from. For example:

.uk means the United Kingdom   **.au** means Australia

.za means South Africa   **.de** means Germany

.es means Spain   **.ca** means Canada

Creating a hyperlink

To make a link in an HTML page, we need to use the anchor tag: **<a>** and **</a>**.

Single straight quotes

<a href='http://www.google.com'>Google</a>

The URL of the site we are linking to

The text that the user will click

Don't forget the **http://** at the start of the URL.

Try it out:

Open up your text editor. For instructions, see page 7.

In your text editor, type:

Text editor

```
<html>
    <a href='http://www.google.com'>Google</a>
</html>
```

Save your file as **mylinks.html**.

Find your file called **mylinks.html** and double-click it.

mylinks.html

You should now see your page in a web browser.

Browser

//desktop/mylinks.html

Google

When you move your mouse over the link it should turn into a finger. Try clicking the link.

Browser

http://www.google.com

Make sure your file name ends in **.html** or it won't work!

Click the **backward arrow** to go back to your page.

11

LOTS OF LINKS

What sites will you choose?

Now we know how hyperlinks work, we are going to build a page that has links to a number of different websites. We will use heading and paragraph tags to add other text to our page.

My favorite sites

1

Open your text editor. If you've forgotten how, turn to page 7.

2

In your text editor, type:

Text editor

```
<html>
    <h1>My Favorite Sites</h1>
    <p>Click one of these:</p>
</html>
```

3

Save your file as **mypages.html** then double-click it to test it so far.

mypages.html

Click **"File"** then **"Save"** after any changes.

4

Arrange your desktop so you have your text editor on the left of the screen and your web browser on the right.

Press **"Refresh"** to see the changes.

Text editor—mypages.html

```
<html>
    <h1>My Favorite Sites</h1>
    <p>Click one of these:</p>
</html>
```

Browser

//desktop/mypages.html

My Favorite Sites

Click one of these:

5

Add a new anchor tag with a favorite website to your HTML page.

Save and refresh your page to test it.

Text editor—mypages.html

```
<html>
    <h1>My Favorite Sites</h1>
    <p>Click one of these:</p>
    <a href='http://www.google.com'>Google</a>
</html>
```

mypages.html

6

Add a second anchor tag and website, then save and refresh your page to test it.

Text editor—mypages.html

```
<html>
    <h1>My Favorite Sites</h1>
    <p>Click one of these:</p>
    <a href='http://www.google.com'>Google</a>
    <a href='http://www.si.edu'>Smithsonian</a>
</html>
```

Ooooh, interesting sites!

Your web page should look like this now.

Browser

//desktop/mypages.html

My Favorite Sites

Click one of these:
Google   Smithsonian

Click the links to test your HTML. If it works, add more links. Ask an adult to check the content of the sites before adding links.

If you want each link to start on a new line, you can add the line break tag: **
**.

```
<a href='http://www.google.com'>Google</a>
<br>
<a href='http://www.giantpandazoo.com'>pandas</a>
<br>
<a href='http://www.si.edu'>Smithsonian</a>
```

Using a more advanced text editor

You can keep using Notepad or TextEdit to make HTML pages for now. (If you're using a Mac, you may have problems with quote marks. Make sure you disable "smart quotes" if you do use TextEdit to make bigger HTML pages—turn to page 31 for help.)

There are lots of programs that can help you make web pages, but to learn HTML and the other web technologies, you need a text editor that lets you stay in control of the code you type.

A text editor that is designed to help you code in HTML will do extra things to help you. It will change the color of different parts of your code so it is easier to check. It will also make sure you have all the tags typed properly.

Sublime Text is a useful text editor that you can download and try out for free. Take a look at: **www.sublimetext.com**. See page 31 for more information about downloading it.

COLOR IT!

We have found out how to add text and links onto a web page. Now we're going to learn how to change the color of them. We will also meet the **<body>** tag, which holds all the things on the page together.

Colored text

1 Start a new web page in your text editor. Type in:

```
Text editor

<html>
    <h1>Web</h1>
    <p>Tim Berners-Lee</p>
</html>
```

2 Save your file as **color.html** then double-click it to test it so far.

color.html

3 Arrange your desktop so you have your text editor on the left of the screen and your web browser on the right.

Click **"File"** then **"Save"** after any changes.

```
Text editor—color.html

<html>
    <h1>Web</h1>
    <p>Tim Berners-Lee</p>
```

```
Browser
◀▶  //desktop/color.html          ↻

Web

Tim Berners-Lee
```

Press the **"Refresh"** button to see any changes.

4 Edit the second line so it looks like this:

```
Text editor—color.html

<html>
    <h1 style='color:red'>Web</h1>
    <p>Tim Berners-Lee</p>
</html>
```

Now save and refresh your page:

```
Browser
◀▶  //desktop/color.html          ↻
Web
Tim Berners-Lee
```

Experiment by typing orange, blue, and other colors instead of red.

5 Edit the third line so it looks like this. What happens?

```
Text editor—color.html

<html>
    <h1 style='color:red'>Web</h1>
    <p style='color:green'>Tim Berners-Lee</p>
</html>
```

Changing the background color

To change the color of the page, first we need to add a **<body>** tag to our HTML.

It's a masterpiece!

The start of the body of the page

The end of the body of the page

Text editor—color.html

```
<html>
   <body>
      <h1 style='color:red'>Web</h1>
      <p style='color:green'>Tim Berners-Lee</p>
   </body>
</html>
```

Now we can add the style "attribute" to set the background color:

Text editor—color.html

```
<html>
   <body style='background-color:yellow'>
      <h1 style='color:red'>Web</h1>
      <p style='color:green'>Tim Berners-Lee</p>
   </body>
</html>
```

Save and refresh. The page should look like this:

Browser

//desktop/color.html

Web

Tim Berners-Lee

Your turn

Now try typing in the HTML below. Check the answers on page 30.

1 Text editor—styles.html

```
<html>
   <h1 style='color:blue'>Tim Berners-Lee</h1>
   <p style='color:orange'>Ada Lovelace</p>
   <p style='color:green'>Alan Turing</p>
</html>
```

Save and refresh to see how each page looks.

2 Text editor—styles.html

```
<html>
   <body style='background-color:black'>
      <p style='color:yellow'>Nelson Mandela</p>
      <p style='color:green'>Mahatma Gandhi</p>
      <p style='color:white'>Rosa Parks</p>
   </body>
</html>
```

ADDING JAVASCRIPT

We've learned how to use basic HTML to choose what goes on a web page. Now we will look at how to add code in a different language: JavaScript. JavaScript decides what the page actually does when we do things like click buttons. It can be used along with HTML.

Click me

1 Start a new web page in your text editor. Type in this HTML:

Text editor
```
<html>
    <button>Click me</button>
</html>
```

2 Save your file as **hello.html** then double-click it to test it so far.

hello.html

Browser
◀▶ //desktop/hello.html ↻

Click me

Try clicking the button . . . Why does nothing happen? We need to tell the button what to do when we click it! To do this we add a "listener." A listener will run JavaScript code when a particular event happens. We are going to use an onclick listener.

3 Now add some JavaScript to your code:

Single quotes around the JavaScript code

Text editor—hello.html
```
<html>
    <button onclick='alert("Hello")'>Click me</button>
</html>
```

Double quotes

If you have smart "sloping" quotes, your code may not work. See page 31.

4 Save and refresh your file to test it.

Browser
◀▶ //desktop/hello.html ↻

Click me

Hello

Key word

Listener: A line of code that is only run when a particular event happens, such as a button being clicked.

Greetings

1 Start a new web page in your text editor. Type in this HTML:

```
Text editor
<html>
  <button>Hello</button>
  <button>Good-bye</button>
</html>
```

2 Save your file as **greetings.html** then double-click it to test it. You should see something like this:

```
Browser
◀ ▶  //desktop/greetings.html          ↻
   [ Hello ]   [ Good-bye ]
```

The buttons are on the page but still need code to make them work.

This time we need to add two onclick listeners—one for each button.

3 Type in the following code, remembering to use single quotes and double quotes carefully—single quotes around the JavaScript, double quotes around the message.

```
Text editor—greetings.html
<html>
  <button onclick='alert("Hello")'>Hello</button>
  <button onclick='alert("Good-bye")'>Good-bye</button>
</html>
```

Challenge

Experiment with changing what is on the buttons and the messages that are displayed. Can you add a third button? What will it show when you click it?

4 Save and refresh your file to test it.

JAVASCRIPT LOOPS

If you have coded in languages like Scratch or Python, you will have come across loops and variables. Loops are sequences of commands that we want the computer to repeat. Variables are values that are stored by a computer. We will look at how to use these techniques in JavaScript.

Doing math

1 Start a new page in your text editor. Type in this code:

Text editor
```
<script>
    document.write(10+10);
</script>
```

Save your file as **numbers.html** then double-click it to test it.

numbers.html

2 Arrange your desktop so you have your text editor on the left of the screen and your web browser on the right.

Semicolon at end of the JavaScript

The start of some JavaScript

Text editor—numbers.html
```
<script>
    document.write(10+10);
</script>
```

The end of the JavaScript

Browser
//desktop/numbers.ht   Refresh

20

Click **"File"** then **"Save"** after changes.

document.write means write something to the document—print something on the screen. You need brackets around the number you are printing or calculating.

Now try these

50+40
80-25

Type in these code examples. Save and refresh your page each time to test.
Answers are on page 30.

1 Text editor—numbers.html
```
<script>
    document.write(50+40);
</script>
```

2 Text editor—numbers.html
```
<script>
    document.write(80-25);
</script>
```

Key word

Loop: A sequence of commands repeated a number of times.

Loops and repeating

We can use loops to write something on the screen over and over again by using a "for" loop.

Edit your code so it says:

Check you have typed the code carefully. It should display 123456789.

Text editor – numbers.html

```
<script>
    for(var n=1; n<10; n++)
        document.write(n);
</script>
```

Save and refresh to test!

How does it work?

| **var** means variable. | **n** starts at 1. | **n** stops before 10. | **n++** makes n get bigger. |

```
for(var n=1; n<10; n++)
    document.write(n);
```

This makes a loop using a variable called **n** that starts at 1. It goes up by 1 each loop and writes the value of n on the document. It keeps looping until n gets to 10.

Then try these

Type in these code examples. We are going to use **writeln(n)** rather than **write(n)** to leave a gap between each number. Answers are on page 30.

Make sure you get the semicolons in the right places!

③ Text editor—numbers.html

```
<script>
    for(var n=10; n<20; n++)
        document.writeln(n);
</script>
```

④ Text editor—numbers.html

```
<script>
    for(var n=20; n<40; n++)
        document.writeln(n);
</script>
```

⑤ Text editor—numbers.html

```
<script>
    for(var n=1; n<10; n++)
        document.writeln(10-n);
</script>
```

⑥ Text editor—numbers.html

```
<script>
    for(var n=20; n>0; n--)
        document.writeln(n);
</script>
```

⑦ Make a loop that counts from 1 to 100.

⑧ Make a loop that counts from 1 to 1,000.

JAVASCRIPT FUNCTIONS

We've seen how we can use loops to repeat lines of code using JavaScript. However, there are times when we just want to repeat some parts of our code again, using different values. To do this, we need to create our own commands called functions.

Make a sandwich

In order to understand the idea of functions, imagine you need to teach a robot how to make sandwiches. You could give it instructions on how to make a ham and cheese sandwich, then another set of instructions on how to make a cheese and tomato sandwich . . . and so on. You would end up writing lots of instructions.

I can make any sandwich now! What would you like?

I'm never going to remember all this!

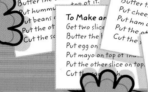

To Make a ... and Bean Sandwich:
... bread.
Butter the bread.
Put hummus ... top of it.
...t beans ...
Put the ot...
Cut the s...

To Make a...
Get two slice...
Butter the b...
Put egg on ...
Put mayo on top of the...
Put the other slice on top.
Cut the sandwich.

To Make a Cheese and Ham Sa...
Get two slices of bread.
Butter the bread.
Put cheese on top of it.
Put ham on top of...
Put the ot...
Cut the s...

To Make a Cheese and Tomato Sandwich:
Get two slices of bread.
Butter the bread.
Put cheese on top of it.
Put tomato on top of that.
Put the other slice on top.
Cut the sandwich.

To Make a Sandwich with (filling2, filling2):
Get two slices of bread.
Butter the bread.
Put **filling1** on top of it.
Put **filling2** on top of that.
Put the other slice on top.
Cut the sandwich.

Instead we could tell our robot how to make any sandwich. Since we don't know what fillings we will need, we will just name them "filling1" and "filling2." We will then write a general sandwich instruction that can be used over and over again, like a function.

NOW INSTEAD OF SAYING:

NOW INSTEAD OF SAYING:	. . . WE WOULD NEED TO SAY:
Make a cheese and tomato sandwich	Make a sandwich with ("cheese", "tomato").
Make a hummus and bean sandwich	Make a sandwich with ("hummus", "bean").

Make a quiz

We are going to make a quiz program. We need to write code to ask a question, then check if it is correct or not, then tell the player. It could look like this:

Key word

Function: A sequence of commands that performs a specific task every time the function is "called."

```
<script>
    var answer=prompt("What is 5 x 5?");
    if(answer=="25") alert("Good job");
    else alert("Wrong");

    var answer=prompt("What is 10 x 10?");
    if(answer=="100") alert("Good job");
    else alert("Wrong");

    var answer=prompt("What is 3 x 3?");
    if(answer=="9") alert("Good job");
    else alert("Wrong");
</script>
```

This line asks for an input and stores the response in a variable called **answer**.

This checks whether the answer is correct and shows "Good job" if it is.

If the answer is not correct, it shows "Wrong."

This works but each question needs 3 lines of code. We need a quicker way!

Instead of repeating 3 lines of code for each question, we can create a function called **ask**. The function will be "called" (run) every time we want to ask a question.

This line starts defining the **ask** function.

Type the curly brackets correctly: **{** and **}**.

```
<script>
    function ask(question, correct){
        var answer=prompt(question);
        if(answer==correct) alert("Good job");
        else alert("Wrong");
    }

    ask("What is 5 x 5","25");
    ask("What is 10 x 10","100");
    ask("What is 3 x 3","9");
</script>
```

The function uses similar code to before, but instead of using words like "What is 3 x 3?"' it uses a variable called **question**.

These lines ask the questions. They "call" the function and pass it values to use as each question and answer.

① Start a new page in your text editor. Type in the JavaScript code above.

② Save your file as **quiz.html** then double-click it to test it.

③ Now add more questions of your own using the **ask** function.

JS FUNCTIONS WITH HTML

We've seen how JavaScript functions can be used to code a simple linear program. "Linear" means the functions run one after another. We are now going to learn to make different functions run when different buttons are clicked.

Changing color

We are going to make a web page that can change color when different buttons are clicked. To start with, we are going to make a page with a button on it, and a function to change the page colour. Finally we will make the function run when the button is clicked.

1 Start a new web page in your text editor. Type in this JavaScript:

Text editor

```
<script>
  function red(){
     document.body.style.backgroundColor="red";
  }
</script>
```

2 Save your file as **change.html** then double-click it to test it so far.

3 Arrange your desktop so you have your text editor on the left of the screen and your web browser on the right.

Text editor—change.html

```
<script>
  function red(){
     document.body.style.backgroundColor="red";
  }
</script>
```

Browser

◀▶

Refresh

4 Edit your file:

Add an **<html>** tag.

Add a button that will call the **red()** function.

Add an **</html>** tag.

Text editor—change.html

```
<html>
<button onclick="red()">Go red</button>
<script>
  function red(){
     document.body.style.backgroundColor="red";
  }
</script>
</html>
```

5 Save and test your file. Click the **"Go red"** button and the page should change!

More colors, more functions?

It would be great if we could add lots more buttons to change the page to other colors. But that would mean adding a separate function for each color. Instead we could make a general "change background color" function named **setbg**. We could "pass" it a color like we passed fillings to the sandwich function on page 20.

We would "call" (run) the function like this: **setbg('red')** or **setbg('blue')** and so on.

1 Start a new web page in your text editor. Type in:

Text editor

```
<script>
  function setbg(col){
    document.body.style.backgroundColor=col;
  }
</script>
```

2 Edit your file:

Add an **<html>** tag.

Add a **button** that will call the **setbg()** function.

Add an **</html>** tag.

Text editor

```
<html>
  <button onclick="setbg('blue')">Go blue</button>
  <script>
    function setbg(col){
      document.body.style.backgroundColor=col;
    }
  </script>
</html>
```

3 Save your file as **colors.html** then double-click it to test it so far.

4 Edit your file:

Go blue   Go green

Insert a new **button** here. Make it call the **setbg()** function.

Text editor—colors.html

```
<html>
<button onclick="setbg('blue')">Go blue</button>
<button onclick="setbg('green')">Go green</button>
<script>
  function setbg(col){
    document.body.style.backgroundColor=col;
  }
</script>
</html>
```

Try adding more buttons to change to other colors . . .

Remember to type everything carefully.

5 Save and test your file. Click the buttons and the page should change color!

PETS PROJECT

Most websites have more than one page. Each page is linked together so anyone using the site can move from page to page. We are going to make a simple site with pages about different animals. We will only be using HTML.

1 Start a new web page in your text editor. Type in this HTML:

Text editor

```
<html>
  <h1>Animals</h1>
</html>
```

2 Make a new folder for your project called **"Animals."** Save your file in it, calling it **index.html**.

3 Open the **Animals** folder and double-click the **index.html** file to test it.

index.html

4 Arrange your desktop so you have the Animals folder, your text editor and your browser all visible at once.

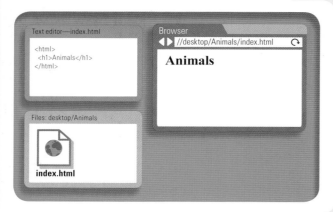

Text editor—index.html
```
<html>
  <h1>Animals</h1>
</html>
```

Browser
//desktop/Animals/index.html

Animals

Files: desktop/Animals
index.html

To make a new folder on a Mac, click **"File," "Save"** and **"New Folder."**

On a PC, right-click in the **Save** box, click **"New"** and **"Folder."**

5 In your text editor, click **"File"** and **"New"** to start the next page. Type in this HTML:

```
<html>
  <h1>Dogs</h1>
</html>
```

Save this one as **dogs.html** in the **Animals** folder.

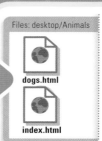

Files: desktop/Animals
dogs.html
index.html

We now have two pages. The next task is to link these pages together. For a reminder about making links, see pages 12 and 13.

Ask an adult before you search for photos on the web.

6 Edit your **index.html** file by adding a link to the **dogs.html** page:

Text editor—index.html

```html
<html>
 <h1>Animals</h1>
 <a href="dogs.html">Dogs</a>
</html>
```

7 Refresh the page:

Browser
//desktop/Animals/index

Animals
<u>Dogs</u>

Click the **"Dogs"** link ...

Browser
//desktop/Animals/dogs

Dogs

8 Repeat Step 5 to create another new file. Save it in the **Animals** folder as **cats.html**.

```html
<html>
 <h1>Cats</h1>
</html>
```

9 Add another link to your **index.html** page to link it to the new **cats.html** page.

Add a **
** to make a line break and space out the links.

Text editor—index.html

```html
<html>
 <h1>Animals</h1>
 <a href="dogs.html">Dogs</a>
 <br>
 <a href="cats.html">Cats</a>
</html>
```

10 Add more information about each animal on its page. Use **<p>** paragraph **</p>** tags around the information. Look back at page 14 to change the colors of pages and text.

Type the file name carefully. If the file is a photo, it will probably end in .jpg.

Adding photos and pictures

To add photos or pictures to your Animals website, you could use your own digital photos of your pets.

Alternatively, you can download pictures from the web. If you're going to display your website online, make sure you use photos that are not covered by copyright. If you're only going to show your website to classmates and family, you don't have to worry about copyright. For more information on copyright, see page 27.

Files: desktop/Animals

dogs.html   cats.html

Add your photo to the **Animals** folder.

Text editor—fish.html

```html
<html>
 <h1>Fish</h1>
 <img src="fish.jpg">
</html>
```

Add an **<img>** (image) tag to display your photo.

Type the file name of the photo after **src=** and between double quotes. Src is short for source.

Browser
//desktop/Animals/fish.html

Fish

SHARING YOUR WEBSITE

Once you have built a website or project on your computer, you may want to share it with other people. To do this you need to load it onto a special computer called a server, which can share it with the world. Make sure you get permission from a parent, guardian, or teacher first.

Website builders

There is lots of software to help people create their own websites, without having to do their own HTML coding. If you just want to make a website about a hobby, these easy-to-use "website builders" are a good option—but you won't learn much about coding! If you search for "website builders" you'll get a list of sites, some with free options. Make sure you ask an adult before you sign up.

1 HTML CONVENTIONS

In this book, we have used the shortest and simplest way to introduce you to HTML. Once you start sharing web pages, you need to follow standard conventions. Make sure all your pages have **<!DOCTYPE html>** at the start. Also include a title tag with the page title, for example: **<title>My web page</title>**. You should always include **<body>** tags (see page 15). Advanced coders include their style information in separate files (called CSS files) and their JavaScript in separate files, too. However, it is fine to use them within your HTML (called "inline" to get started). For more information on web standards, visit: **http://www.w3.org**.

2 TEST YOUR SITE

Before you share your site, you need to test it to make sure it works properly on your computer. Read through your text and look for any spelling mistakes or missing punctuation marks. Ask a friend if they can use the site on your computer. Do the page titles and links make sense? Have you used colors that make the page easy to read?

3 E-SAFETY

If you are going to share your site on the web, anyone will be able to read it. Think carefully about any information or images you put on the pages, and always get permission from an adult. You should follow these rules, and any other rules about e-safety that you have at home and school:

- Don't share personal information—such as your full name, address, or email address.
- Don't include photos of you or your family.
- Don't write anything unkind about other people on your site.

4 COPYRIGHT

Before you use photos or other images on your website, make sure you have permission to include them. If you download a photo from another website, make sure it is "copyright free" or has been shared under a "creative commons licence." You should always credit the photographer.

You will be able to include a picture you have drawn in a painting program, or scanned onto your computer. If you have taken a photo of something (not someone!), then you will also be able to use it on your site.

5 WEBSPACE

You need to copy your website onto a special computer called a server that will host your website. The place to do this on the server is called webspace. You may have some free webspace provided as part of your internet or broadband access. If not, search online for "webspace" or "web hosting." You can get free webspace or pay for your website to be hosted. You will need to pay more if you want a special website address. However, check with an adult before you do any of this.

6 UPLOADING

To upload your website, you need to use a special piece of software called an FTP program. FTP stands for File Transfer Protocol. It enables you to transfer the HTML files in your project folder from your computer to the server. You can download a free FTP program called FileZilla from **https://filezilla-project.org/**. See page 31 for more information.

You will need to enter login and password information from your web host.

Your website will now be live! Check it works OK. If there are any problems, fix them on your computer first, changing the files in your project folder. Then drag the files across to the remote site using the FTP program.

Drag files from the local folder to the remote folder on the right.

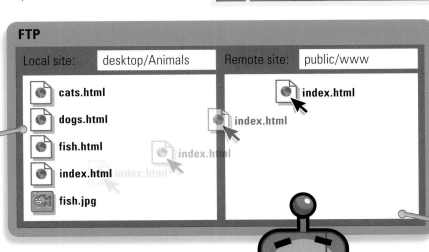

FTP

| Local site: | desktop/Animals | Remote site: | public/www |

cats.html
dogs.html
fish.html
index.html
fish.jpg

index.html
index.html

Browse your project folder on the left of the FTP program.

Ask permission from an adult before you upload to a website.

DEBUGGING

Coding can be a process of trial and error—testing ideas and seeing if they work. It is usual to make mistakes doing this. A bug is another name for a mistake in a piece of code that stops it working properly. Debugging means fixing those mistakes. Try these exercises then check your answers on page 30.

1

This HTML page needs to show each piece of fruit on a separate line . . .

Text editor—fruit.html

```
<html>
  <p>Apple</p>
  Banana
  Cranberry
  Date
</html>
```

. . . but it doesn't:

Browser

//desktop/fruit.html

Apple
Banana Cranberry Date

Debug it!

Debugging tips

When your code doesn't do what you want it to:

1 Check you have all the tags, colons, brackets, and quotes you need and that they match.

2 Go through your code step by step, thinking about what each command and tag does.

3 Draw a picture or diagram to help.

4 Have a break for a few minutes!

2

This HTML should link to Google when it is clicked. But which version has no bugs: A, B, C, or D? Why?

A
```
<html>
  <p>Click on a link:</p>
  <a href='http://www.google.com'>Google</a>
</html>
```

B
```
<html>
  <p>Click on a link:</p>
  <a href='Google'>http://www.google.com</a>
</html>
```

C
```
<html>
  <p>Click on a link:</p>
  <a href='http://www.google.com>Google</a>
</html>
```

D
```
<html>
  <p>Click on a link:</p>
  <a href='http://www.google.com'></a>Google
</html>
```

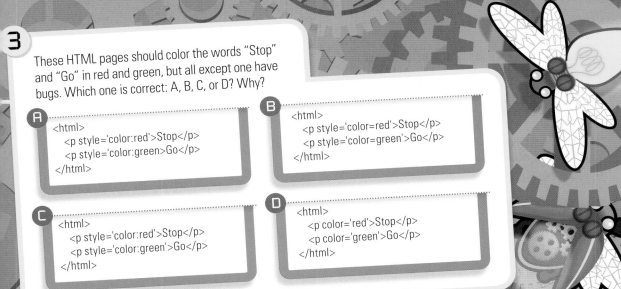

3

These HTML pages should color the words "Stop" and "Go" in red and green, but all except one have bugs. Which one is correct: A, B, C, or D? Why?

A
```
<html>
  <p style='color:red'>Stop</p>
  <p style='color:green'>Go</p>
</html>
```

B
```
<html>
  <p style='color=red'>Stop</p>
  <p style='color=green'>Go</p>
</html>
```

C
```
<html>
  <p style='color:red'>Stop</p>
  <p style='color:green'>Go</p>
</html>
```

D
```
<html>
  <p color='red'>Stop</p>
  <p color='green'>Go</p>
</html>
```

4

This JavaScript should count from 1 all the way to 10 . . .

. . . but it doesn't:

Text editor—counting.html
```
<script>
 for(var n=1; n<10; n++)
   document.writeln(n);
</script>
```

Browser
//desktop/counting.html

1 2 3 4 5 6 7 8 9

Debug it!

Coding guidelines

Think about these guidelines when you are coding:

1 Plan your program carefully, either with a diagram or some notes.

2 When you are learning to code, it is better to write lots of small, simple programs rather than one larger and more complex program.

3 Test your program as you build it: don't wait until you have put all the commands in.

5

This JavaScript should count from 30 to 50 . . .

. . . but it doesn't!

Text editor – numbers.html
```
<script>
 for(var n=30; n<50; n++)
   document.writeln(30);
</script>
```

Browser
//desktop/numbers.html

30 30 30 30 30 30 30 30 30 30 30 30 30 30 30 30 30 30 30 30

Can you debug it?

ANSWERS

Page 9

1

Browser
//desktop/headings

Cyber Cafe

Open every day

2

Browser
//desktop/headings

Code School

Smith Street

Learn to code

3

Browser
//desktop/headings

Huge

Medium

Tiny

4

Browser
//desktop/headings

London

England

Paris

France

Page 15

1

Browser
//desktop/styles.html

Tim Berners-Lee

Ada Lovelace

Alan Turing

2

Browser
//desktop/styles.html

Nelson Mandela

Mahatma Gandhi

Rosa Parks

Pages 18–19

1 90   **2** 55   **3** 10 11 12 13 14 15 16 17 18 19

4 20 21 22 23 ... 35 36 37 38 39   **5** 9 8 7 6 5 4 3 2 1

6 20 19 18 17 16 15 14 13 12 11 10 9 8 7 6 5 4 3 2 1

7

Text editor—numbers.html

```
<script>
 for(var n=1; n<101; n++)
  document.writeln(n);
</script>
```

8

Text editor—numbers.html

```
<script>
 for(var n=1; n<1001; n++)
  document.writeln(n);
</script>
```

Page 28–29

1 missing **<p>** and **</p>** tags around Banana, Cranberry, and Date

2 **A** correct

B the URL and **'Google'** are switched around

C missing quote after the URL

D **</a>** should be after **Google**

3 **A** missing quote after **green**

B **'color=red'** should be **'color:red'**

C correct

D color='red' should be style='color:red'

4 **n<10** should be **n<11** or **n<=10**

5 two mistakes:
n<50 should be **n<=50** or **n<51**
document.writeln(30); should be **document.writeln(n);**

INFORMATION ON RESOURCES

TEXT EDITORS FOR HTML AND JAVASCRIPT

Before you start coding, you'll need a suitable text editor. Most computers will already have a text editor. On a PC, you'll find **Notepad**. On a Mac, you'll find **TextEdit**. These are fine for basic HTML.

SPECIALIST HTML EDITORS

If you intend to take your coding to the next level, you'll find that using a dedicated HTML editor will make things easier. A text editor that is designed to help you code in HTML will change the color of your code to make it easier to check, and make sure you have all the tags typed properly. **Sublime Text** is a very useful text editor that you can download and try for free. You will probably find Sublime Text useful for the activities from page 14 onward. To download it, go to:
www.sublimetext.com

FTP PROGRAMS

If you are going to upload HTML files to create a public website, you will need an FTP program to transfer the files. You can use **FileZilla** to do this for free.
To download it, go to: **https://filezilla-project.org/.**

Choose to download the **"Client"** version, not the "Server" version.

After downloading FileZilla, the first time you run it you will need to set it up. To do this you need to click **"File"** then **"Site manager"** and enter various pieces of information. This will include username, password and the address of the site. This information should be provided by your web host.

ON A MAC: USING TEXTEDIT

If you are working with TextEdit, first of all click the **"TextEdit"** menu, then click **"Preferences."**

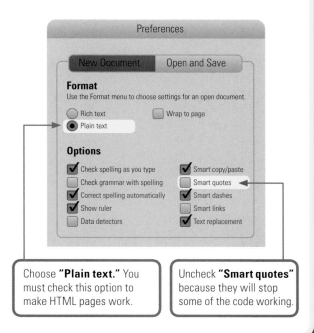

Choose **"Plain text."** You must check this option to make HTML pages work.

Uncheck **"Smart quotes"** because they will stop some of the code working.

Other books in the *How to Code* series:

BOOK 1

Introduction to the basic principles of coding. Experiment with Logo and Scratch. Move turtles and sprites across the screen!
ISBN: 978 1 93958 188 4

BOOK 2

Builds on basic coding and introduces loops and repetition. Code a maze game in Scratch and learn how to add sound effects to a game!
ISBN: 978 1 93958 189 1

BOOK 3

Take coding further by learning about selection with "if" statements. Code a simple quiz in Python or make a sandwich for a robot!
ISBN: 978 1 93958 190 7

GLOSSARY

Attribute Extra information about an object or text, such as its style, font, width, or height.

Browser A program used to view websites and HTML pages. Popular browsers include Chrome, Firefox, Internet Explorer, and Safari.

Code A set of words, numbers or symbols that tells a computer what to do.

Command A word or set of numbers, and symbols that tells the computer what to do.

Debugging Fixing problems (bugs) in a computer program.

Domain A part of the internet that is made up of computers or websites that are related in some way. For example, they may all be in Canada and have web addresses ending .ca.

Download To copy data from one computer to another using the internet.

Editor (or text editor) A program used to type and edit programs.

Email A system for sending messages from one computer to another using the internet.

Event Something that happens while a program is running; for example a key being pressed, or the program starting.

Function A sequence of commands created to do something such as draw a square every time the function is run or "called."

HTML (Hypertext Markup Language) The language used to define the objects or elements that are on web pages.

HTTP (Hypertext Transfer Protocol) Rules for transporting HTML pages over the internet.

Hyperlink Link to another web page, which can be reached by clicking the mouse or touching a touchscreen.

Indent Using tabs or spaces to move a line of code in from the left.

Input An action (such as pressing a key) that tells a program to do something.

Internet A worldwide network of computers.

JavaScript The programming language used in some web pages to make them more interactive.

Language A system of words, numbers, symbols, and rules for writing programs.

Listener A line of code or function that is only run when a particular event happens, such as a button being clicked.

Loop A sequence of commands repeated a number of times.

Network A group of computers connected by wires or, often, wireless links.

Online Connected to the internet.

Program The special commands that tell a computer how to do something.

Protocol A system of rules.

Server A computer or group of computers that stores and delivers web pages.

Tags Special words used to describe what objects there are on a web page. They are always surrounded by angle brackets <>.

Upload To transfer files from your computer to another computer, which is often larger and in a different place.

URL (Uniform Resource Locator) The address or location of a website or HTML page. It is usually shown at the top of the browser window.

Variable A value or piece of data stored by a program.

Web page A page of information constructed using HTML and connected to the World Wide Web.

Wireless Communicating without connecting wires, often using radio waves.

World Wide Web (or web) A worldwide network of HTML files, which we can access using the internet.

INDEX